D0573875

Russian Foods & Culture

by Jennifer Ferro

The Rourke Press, Inc.

Vero Beach, FL 32964

On the Cover: *Russians buy eggs painted with elaborate decorations for Easter.*

Photo Credits: Cover photo Reuters/Gennady Galperin/Archive Photos; p. 4 EyeWire; p. 6 H. Huntly Hersch; p. 8, 11 Lou Dematteis; p. 12, 22, 32 PhotoDisc; p. 13 AP Photo/Ivan Nikitin; p. 14 Reuters/Peter Morgan/Archive Photos; p. 18, 28, 39 Paul O'Connor; p. 23 AP Photo/Ivan Sekretarev; p. 33 CORBIS/Mark Stephenson.

Produced by Salem Press, Inc.

Library of Congress Cataloging-in-Publication Data

Ferro, Jennifer. 1968-
    Russian foods and culture / Jennifer Ferro.
    p.   cm. — (Festive foods & celebrations)
    Summary: Discusses some of the foods enjoyed in Russia and describes special foods that are part of such specific celebrations as Easter, Pancake Week, and Fish Harvest. Includes recipes.
    ISBN 1-57103-305-X
    1. Cookery, Russian Juvenile literature. 2. Food habits—Russia (Federation) Juvenile literature. 3. Festivals—Russia (Federation) Juvenile literature. [1. Food habits—Russia (Federation) 2. Cookery, Russian. 3. Festivals—Russia (Federation) 4. Holidays—Russia (Federation) 5. Russia (Federation)—Social life and customs.] I. Title. II. Series: Ferro, Jennifer. 1968-   Festive foods & celebrations.
TX723.3.F47   1999
641.5947—dc21   99-21048
                                                                                      CIP

First Printing

PRINTED IN THE UNITED STATES OF AMERICA

Contents

Introduction to Russia

Russia (RUH-shuh) is a large country on the continents (KON-tun-untz) of *Europe* (YUR-up) and *Asia* (AY-zhuh). The western part *borders* Finland and the Baltic Sea. The eastern part reaches to the Pacific Ocean. Russia almost touches Alaska in the United States. People who live in Russia are called Russians (RUH-shunz). Most of them live in the western part of the country.

Siberia (si-BEER-ee-uh) is in eastern Russia. It is one of the coldest places in the world. For six

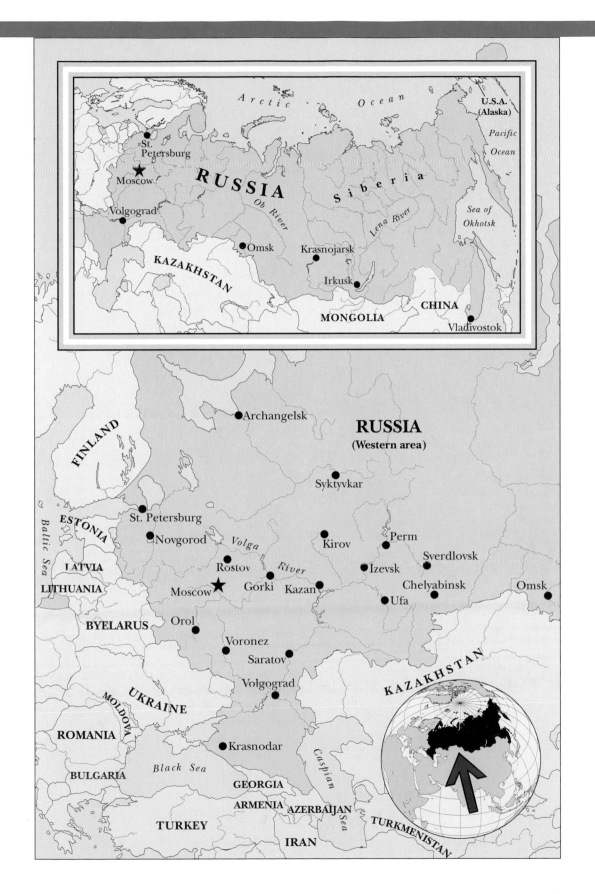

Arctic Ocean

RUSSIA

Siberia

U.S.A. (Alaska)

Pacific Ocean

St. Petersburg

Moscow

Volgograd

Ob River

Lena River

Sea of Okhotsk

KAZAKHSTAN

Omsk

Krasnojarsk

Irkusk

MONGOLIA

CHINA

Vladivostok

Archangelsk

RUSSIA
(Western area)

FINLAND

Syktyvkar

Baltic Sea

ESTONIA

St. Petersburg

Novgorod

Volga

Kirov

Perm

Sverdlovsk

LATVIA

Rostov

River

Izevsk

Chelyabinsk

Omsk

LITHUANIA

Moscow

Gorki

Kazan

Ufa

BYELARUS

Orol

Voronez

KAZAKHSTAN

UKRAINE

Saratov

MOLDOVA

Volgograd

ROMANIA

Krasnodar

Caspian Sea

BULGARIA

Black Sea

GEORGIA

TURKEY

ARMENIA

AZERBAIJAN

TURKMENISTAN

IRAN

5

An old woman hangs up hay to dry. Many Russian peasants still live as people did centuries ago.

months of the year, the sun never comes up. For the rest of the year, it never gets dark. The winters in Siberia last eight months. People who go outside must breathe through fur or cloth masks so their lungs do not freeze.

Russia has a long history. For many years, it was ruled by people from Asia called Mongols. In 1547, Ivan the Terrible became the first czar (ZAR), or Russian *emperor*. Peter the Great founded the Russian Empire in 1721.

Until the early 1900's, most Russians were peasants (PEH-zuntz). Peasants are people who live in small villages. Many of them are farmers who do not own the land. The Russian peasants worked very hard but got little in return. They did not have enough to eat.

In 1917, a group of people called Bolsheviks (BOWL-shuh-vicks) stood up for the peasants. They killed the czar and took over Russia. This was called the Russian Revolution. A revolution is when the rulers of a country are forced out of power. They are replaced by different leaders.

Russia and many other regions together became known as the *Soviet Union* (SOH-vee-ut YOON-yun) or the U.S.S.R. The Communist Party was formed after the revolution. It ruled Russia under a new type of government called *communism* (KAH-myoo-nih-zum). No one could own any property or business. The government owned everything. All people worked for the government.

The Communist Party took care of the people.

Russians had free health care and free education. Prices for food were kept low so everyone could buy it. But there was not enough food. Russians stood in long lines for bread.

Russians could not say anything they wanted. They could not vote for their own leaders. The Communist Party made practicing religion against the law. It was illegal to attend church or to read certain books. People caught doing these things

Some Russians still bring flowers every Sunday to the tomb of communist leader V. I. Lenin.

were arrested. Some of them were exiled (ECK-siled), or forced to leave Russia forever. Others were sent to live in Siberia.

In 1991, the Soviet Union broke up. Now Russians can own businesses and vote in elections. They are allowed to practice religion. Russians celebrate religious holidays like Christmas and Easter. Most Russians belong to a branch of Christianity called the Russian Orthodox Church.

A lot of wheat and other grains are grown in Russia. They are made into bread. Sometimes Russia is called the "breadbasket of Europe." Bread is an important part of eating in Russia.

Russians gather mushrooms in the countryside in the fall—September, October, and November. Sometimes mushrooms are eaten raw. Usually they are *pickled* in vinegar. Russians give pickled mushrooms as a gift. Mushrooms are also dried so they can be eaten later in the year. Mushrooms feel like meat when they are cooked. They can be used when people are not allowed to eat meat.

Most Russians eat a small breakfast of tea with milk and bread. The next meal is called "dinner." The last meal of the day is called "supper."

At a Russian table are salt, pepper, and mustard. There is also a dark bread made from a grain called *rye*. First guests eat cold foods like meat, ham, smoked fish, and cold vegetables. Then they eat a hot soup. Finally they have some fish or meat.

Kasha (KAH-shah) is a national food of Russia. It is eaten for breakfast and dinner. Kasha is made from many grains. It is like oatmeal. Kasha starts out dry and is added to boiling water. It can be made like a liquid. It can also be made thick and sweetened with sugar and fruit.

Russian soldiers take photographs in front of St. Basil's Cathedral in the capital city of Moscow.

Easter

Easter is a holiday that celebrates the story of *Jesus Christ.* Jesus lived two thousand years ago. His teachings about religion made many Jews and Romans angry. He was killed on a cross. This is called the Crucifixion (kroo-suh-FICK-shun). It is remembered on Good Friday.

Christians believe that Jesus rose from the dead after three days. This is called the Resurrection (reh-zuh-RECK-shun). It is celebrated on Easter Sunday. Christians believe that Jesus went to

Heaven. Easter is a time to remember that Jesus watches over everyone in the world.

Easter is an important holiday in Russia. People celebrated Easter even when the Communist Party made it illegal.

Eggs are decorated for Easter. They are *symbols* of birth and life. Russians paint eggs with beautiful

A Russian Orthodox priest blesses kulich for Easter.

Each of these Fabergé eggs is worth more than $100,000.

Easter Eggs

People in many countries decorate eggs for Easter. No one makes more beautiful eggs than Russians do. Russian eggs can be pieces of art. The most famous eggs were those made by Karl Fabergé (fah-bur-ZHAY). Fabergé designed things like jewelry. In 1884, Czar Alexander III asked him to make a special Easter egg for the czar's wife. The egg was made of gold. Inside the egg was a *yolk* made of gold. Inside the yolk was a small golden hen. Inside the hen was a copy of the czar's crown made of diamonds. Fabergé eggs are still very expensive. They can be seen in museums around the world.

colors. They turn ordinary eggs into objects of art. People give painted eggs to friends and family as Easter gifts.

A special Easter cake called kulich (KOO-lick) is baked. This tall cake looks like the hat worn by Russian Orthodox *priests.* Years ago, kulich was baked one week before the holiday. People walked around the church with it. The cake was cut after midnight on Easter. All the members of the church ate it. Russians still make kulich but now they eat it at home.

On the day before Easter, Russians pack eggs, sausage, cheese, ham, butter, and bread into a basket. They take the basket to church. The priests say a *blessing* over the food. The people take it home to be eaten the next day.

Russians go to church at midnight on Easter. They cannot eat anything that day. They are very hungry when they come home. People are ready to eat the big feast that everyone has been preparing all week.

Another special Easter food is a dessert called pashka (POSH-kah). It is made with cheese in lumps called curd. This dessert is in the shape of a *pyramid*. The letters *X* and *B* are made with candy on the side of the pyramid. These letters stand for "Christ is risen."

On Easter, Russians kiss each other three times and say, "Christ is risen." The answer back is "Yes, he has risen."

Stuffed Eggs

6 eggs

2 tablespoons of mayonnaise

1 tablespoon of Dijon mustard

2 tablespoons of sweet pickle relish

salt and pepper

paprika

- Place the eggs in a large saucepan. Cover them with water. Bring to a *boil* on high heat. Boil for 10 minutes.

- Pour out the water. Run cold water over the eggs. Set them aside.

- Mix the mayonnaise, Dijon mustard, relish, and a sprinkle of salt and pepper in a bowl.

- Gently crack the eggs open when they are cool. Peel off the shells. Cut the eggs in half lengthwise.

- Remove the egg yolks. Press on them with a fork to break them up. Blend them into the mixture.

- Place the 12 egg halves on a plate. Spoon 1 teaspoon of the mixture into each place where the yolk was. Sprinkle with paprika. Serves 6.

Stuffed Eggs

Kulich

This Easter cake is supposed to be very tall. You can use a large coffee can as the cake mold. Cut off the top with a can opener. Stand the coffee can up in a cake pan.

Cake

1 stick of unsalted butter

1 tablespoon of active dry yeast

1 cup of milk

1 cup of sugar

2 eggs

3 cups of flour

1/3 cup of raisins

1 tablespoon of mixed dried fruit

salt

2 drops of vanilla extract

◆ Warm the milk. Dissolve the yeast in the milk in a large bowl.

- Melt the butter. Add the sugar, eggs, and butter to the milk. Mix with an electric mixer.

- Leave the dough in a warm place for 4 hours to let the yeast rise.

- Fold in the flour with a spatula. Add the raisins, dried fruit, a sprinkle of salt, and vanilla.

- Dust flour on your hands and on a cutting board. Form the dough into a ball. Push into it with your fists. Fold the edges into the center.

- Spray the coffee can and cake pan with nonstick cooking spray. Cut out a circle of wax paper to fit into the bottom of the can.

- Place the dough into the coffee can. Leave it on the counter for 1 hour to let it rise to the top.

- Preheat the oven to 350 degrees. Bake for 45 minutes. Let the cake cool before removing it.
- Pour icing on top (see the following recipe). Serve.

Icing

1/2 cup of powdered sugar
3 drops of vanilla extract
1 egg
2 tablespoons of warm water

- Pour the sugar and vanilla into a bowl.
- Crack the egg into another bowl. Use an egg separator to separate the yolk from the egg white.
- Add the egg white and warm water to the sugar and vanilla.
- Use a whisk to beat the mixture into an icing.

May Day

Russians celebrate this holiday on May 1st. It started many years ago as a festival to mark the beginning of spring. Then it was known as May Day.

In May Day festivals, people danced around the *maypole*. This pole was decorated with flowers and colorful strings. Girls and boys held hands in a circle around the pole. On this day, a May Day queen was chosen. There was dancing and feasting.

Folk dancers celebrate May Day in Moscow.

This festival changed after the Communist Party came to power. In 1886, police officers killed workers in Chicago, Illinois. This shooting is remembered every May 1st all over the world.

The Communist Party named this holiday International Workers Day. It is a time to remember working people. In some countries, it is called Labor Day.

The holiday changed again when the Communist Party lost power. In Russia, May 1st is now called Spring Holiday. It is more like the *traditional* May Day festival.

Vodka

Every adult in Russia drinks tea and vodka. Vodka is a kind of *alcohol* made from rye. It is very strong. Many Russians have vodka with every meal except breakfast. They drink it in tiny glasses after eating dishes like pickles and bread or Russian pancakes. Drinking vodka is a sign of friendship in Russia. But too much can make a person sick.

Cabbage

Cabbage is a vegetable with green leaves. A head of cabbage can weight up to 7 pounds. Cabbage can grow in cold climates. Maybe that is why it is one of the few vegetables that Russians eat often. Russians make a soup out of cabbage called shchi (SHEE). This soup tastes good because it uses sour cabbage. Sour cabbage has been pickled in vinegar and salt. Shchi also has potatoes and carrots in it. It is served with sour cream or milk and rye bread.

Russians still see this day as a chance to be with friends and family. No Russian is without a cake and some flowers to help celebrate.

Babka
(mashed potatoes)

4 russet potatoes
1/4 cup of milk
3 tablespoons of butter
salt

- Peel the potatoes. Cut into cubes. Put them into a saucepan. Cover with water. Turn the heat on high. Bring the water to a boil.

- Turn the heat down to medium. Cook for about 10 minutes, until a fork slides through the potatoes easily.

- Pour out most of the water. Leave about 1 inch in the pan. Stir the potatoes into a paste with a hand-held mixer or a masher.

- Add the milk slowly. The potatoes will be runny if you add too much! Stir.

- Add the butter. Let it melt. Stir.

- Add some salt. Serves 4.

Straw Potatoes

4 large russet potatoes
2 cups of vegetable oil
salt

- Peel the potatoes. Cut into slices 1/4-inch thick. Cut these long slices into 1/4-inch strips. This makes French fries. Cut them thinner if you want smaller strips like hash browns.

- Pour the oil into a saucepan over medium heat. Drop a small piece of potato into the oil. Start adding the rest when it turns golden brown and crispy.

♦ Add small amounts of the potatoes at a time. Putting in too many at once will lower the temperature of the oil. The potatoes will not get crispy.

Straw Potatoes

Vegetable Salad

1/2 head of cabbage

1 bunch of radishes

2 cucumbers

1/2 of a brown onion

8 ounces of feta cheese or 4 ounces of
large curd cottage cheese

1 1/2 cups of sour cream

1 tablespoon of olive oil

salt

◆ *Shred* the cabbage.

◆ Cut off the root ends and tops of the radishes. Throw them away. Cut the radishes into thin slices.

◆ Peel the cucumbers. Cut off the ends and throw them away. Cut the cucumbers into slices as thin as the radishes.

- Cut the onion in half. Peel off the skin and outer layer. Chop an onion half into thin slices.

- Break up the feta cheese so it crumbles into a mixing bowl. Or add the cottage cheese to the bowl.

- Mix in the radishes, cucumbers, cabbage, and onion. Add the oil and sour cream. Stir to coat the vegetables.

- Sprinkle a little salt on top. Stir. Serves 6.

Kompot
(a fruit drink)

1/4 pound of raspberries
1/2 pound of strawberries

1/4 pound of blueberries

6 cups of water

1 cup of sugar

1/8 teaspoon of nutmeg

6 cinnamon sticks

- Put the fruit and water in a large saucepan over high heat. Bring it to a boil. Turn the heat down to *simmer*.

- Add the sugar. Stir until it dissolves.

- Add the nutmeg. Let the mixture simmer for 10 minutes.

- Let it cool down a little. Put one cinnamon stick into each glass. Pour the mixture into the glasses. Serve this drink hot. Serves 6.

Pancake Week

The Russian festival of maslenitsa (moss-len-IT-zuh) is also called Pancake Week or Butter Week. It comes right before the religious season of Lent. Lent lasts for 40 days and ends on Easter.

Lent is a time when people fast. Fasting means not eating anything or not eating certain foods. During Lent, Russians cannot eat meat and dairy products like sour cream, milk, and butter. They eat these foods during Pancake Week

Caviar

Caviar (KAV-ee-are) is salted fish eggs that come from a fish called a sturgeon (STIR-jun). In Russia and around the world, caviar is a *delicacy* (DEH-lih-kuh-see). Even a small amount can cost hundreds of dollars. Russian caviar comes from fish in the Caspian Sea or the Black Sea. The eggs can be gold, black, brown, dark green, or gray. They are washed in cold water and sorted by size and color. Then the eggs are salted and placed in metal containers. The amount of salt sets the price. Many people who taste caviar for the first time are surprised by how salty it is. They are probably eating less expensive caviar. The most expensive kind has the least amount of salt. In Russia, caviar is usually eaten on a cracker or a blini with some sour cream.

Caviar

because they will have to give them up for the next 40 days.

Today Pancake Week is related to Easter. But holidays in Russia were different before people followed the Russian Orthodox religion. Festivals were based on the *seasons*.

Maslenitsa used to celebrate the end of a long winter and the beginning of spring. Spring is a special season. It is a time when plants grow again after a cold winter. Spring is also a time when the weather is warmer. The sun is in the sky longer.

Many years ago, people wore funny masks and costumes during maslenitsa. Men and women dressed up in each other's clothing.

Before communism, this festival was a big public party. Russians stayed up until late at night. In the Soviet Union, it was celebrated mainly in people's homes. Now Russians can celebrate in public again. But Pancake Week is still not an official holiday.

A figure called the Man of Winter is made of straw. It is burned during Pancake Week as a final act of saying good-bye to winter.

The best part of this holiday is eating pancakes! Pancakes are symbols for the sun. In ancient times, pancakes were offered to the dead around this time of year.

Many different types of pancakes are made.

The Fish Harvest

Many years ago, Russians strictly followed the holidays of the Russian Orthodox Church. There were many fasts during the year. Over 200 out of 365 days of the year were fasting days. During a fast, Russians could not eat meat, milk, eggs, cream, or butter. One fast started two weeks after Easter. It lasted until the end of June. People were allowed to eat fish during this fast. People in towns along the *Volga River* were asked to catch fish. They were paid with fish for their help. Today, people no longer help with the fish *harvest*. Also, pollution in the Volga River has killed many of the fish.

They are called blinis (BLEE-neez). A blini is soft and fluffy. It is like a sponge that soaks up anything it is served with.

Everyone loves pancakes in Russia—from the richest people to the poorest. Some Russians come home from work to have pancakes for dinner. These pancakes are served with butter, sour cream, jam, and fish. People make sandwiches out of the pancakes too.

Anything can be eaten on a pancake. Try your own toppings!

Blinis

2 cups of buttermilk or whole milk

4 cups of flour

1 egg

1/2 teaspoon of salt

1 tablespoon of sugar

1 tablespoon of dry yeast

1 tablespoon of vegetable oil

◆ Warm the buttermilk.

◆ Scoop the flour into a large mixing bowl. Stir as you pour in the warm buttermilk. Press out all the lumps.

◆ Dissolve the yeast in 1/8 cup of warm water.

◆ Add the egg, salt, sugar, and yeast mixture. Stir. The batter should drop off a fork slower than water but not like a paste. Stir in 1/4 cup of warm water if it seems too thick.

◆ Let the batter sit in a warm place for about 15 minutes.

◆ Heat a small frying pan on medium. Add the oil. Drop in a little batter. Wait until it sizzles. For bigger pancakes, pour enough batter into the pan to cover the bottom. You can make them any size you want.

◆ Flip the pancake with a spatula when it lifts around the edges. Peek underneath with a spatula when the other side starts to lift. Move the pancake to a plate if it

is evenly golden brown. Cover to
keep warm.

◆ Repeat until the batter is gone.
Serve with sour cream, jam, and
butter. Serves 4.

Blinis

Strawberry Kisel
(an after-dinner fruit drink)

1 pound of frozen strawberries
1/2 cup of cornstarch
8 1/2 cups of water
1 cup of sugar
whipped cream

◆ Pour the strawberries into a
   blender. Mix on crush or chop
   until they are mashed into a pulp.

◆ Put the water and cornstarch
   into a large saucepan. Stir until
   the cornstarch dissolves.

◆ Turn the heat on high. Bring the
   water to a boil.

- Add the strawberries. Stir until the mixture starts to get thick.

- Take the pan off the heat. Let the mixture cool down.

- Refrigerate for about 2 hours, until chilled.

- Pour the drink into cold glasses. Top with a spoonful of whipped cream. Serves 6.

Glossary

alcohol: a drink that is made by fermenting fruits, vegetables, or grains.

Asia: a large continent that has such countries as China, India, and Vietnam.

blessing: an act by a god or religious leader that makes something holy.

boil: to heat water or another liquid until it starts to bubble.

border: the line that marks where one country ends and another begins.

communism: a form of government in which the state owns all the businesses.

continent: a large body of land separated from other bodies of land by an ocean or sea. There are seven continents in the world.

delicacy: something to eat that tastes good and is hard to find.

emperor: the leader of a large group of countries

called an empire.

Europe: a continent with such countries as Italy, France, Germany, Hungary, and Switzerland.

harvest: the time of year when foods are ripe and ready to be picked.

Jesus Christ: the founder of the Western religion called Christianity. He was born near Jerusalem two thousand years ago.

maypole: a tall pole with flowers and ribbons that people dance around during May Day celebrations.

pickled: a food that has been cooked in a vinegar mixture so it can be kept for a long time without spoiling.

priest: a leader in some branches of Christianity, such as the Russian Orthodox Church.

pyramid: a shape made up of four sides that are triangles.

rye: a grass whose seeds are used to flavor bread and other foods.

season: one of the four parts of the year—spring, summer, winter, and fall. Each season has a different kind of weather and different fruits and vegetables that become ripe.

shred: to rip or chop into thin strips.

simmer: to cook on a very low heat.

Soviet Union: also known as U.S.S.R., or Union of Soviet Socialist Republics; the countries that made up the communist states in Asia and Europe.

symbol: something that stands for something else.

traditional: happening the same way for many years.

Volga River: a long river that runs through Russia.

yolk: the yellow part of an egg.

Bibliography

Angell, Carole S. *Celebrations Around the World: A Multicultural Handbook.* Golden, Colo.: Fulcrum Press, 1996.

Harvey, Miles. *Look What Came from Russia.* New York: Franklin Watts, 1999.

Kindersley, Anabel, and Barnabas Kindersley. *Celebrations: Festivals, Carnivals, and Feast Days from Around the World.* New York: DK Publishing, 1997.

Kort, Michael. *Russia.* Rev. ed. New York: Facts on File, 1998.

Perrin, Penelope. *Discovering Russia.* New York: Crestwood House, 1994.

Plotkin, Gregory. *Cooking the Russian Way.* Minneapolis: Lerner Publications, 1986.

Schemenauer, Elma. *Russia.* Chanhassen, Minn.: Child's World, 1999.

Thonnes, Kristin. *Russia.* Mankato. Minn.: Bridgestone Books, 1999.

Torchinsky, Oleg. *Cultures of the World: Russia.* New York: Marshall Cavendish, 1994.

Webb, Lois Sinaiko. *Holidays of the World Cookbook for Students.* Phoenix, Ariz.: Oryx Press, 1995.

websites:

http://www.holidayfestival.com

http://192.204.3.5/Lifestyle/Holidays/winter.html

Index